JOHN DENVER,
AMERICA'S FAVORITE FOLKSINGER!

"I love making records. I love doing television. I love diving in the sea with Captain Jacques Cousteau, climbing mountains and everything. Just about the most meaningful thing in my life is to be upfront of people and share my music with them."

—John Denver

JOHN DENVER

David Dachs

PYRAMID BOOKS
NEW YORK

JOHN DENVER

A PYRAMID BOOK

Pyramid edition published August 1976
Second printing, September, 1976

Library of Congress Catalog Card Number: 76-21945

Printed in the United States of America.

Pyramid Books are published by Pyramid Publications (Harcourt
Brace Jovanovich, Inc.). Its trademarks, consisting of the word
"Pyramid" and the portrayal of a pyramid, are registered in the
United States Patent Office.

PYRAMID PUBLICATIONS
(Harcourt Brace Jovanovich, Inc.)
757 Third Avenue, New York, N.Y. 10017

ACKNOWLEDGMENTS

I wish to thank the following persons and organizations for background material and help in acquiring information and photographs: Julie Dachs, Josh Dachs, Jim Chang, Tricia Heinrich, editor of Texas Tech alumni magazine, *Techsan*; Olga Curtis, *Denver Post*; Edwin Miller, *Seventeen*; Mike Alexander, CBS-TV Publicity; Chet Flippo, *The Rolling Stone*; Walter Wager, ASCAP, Irv Lichtman, Chad Mitchell; Music Theatre Collection of the Lincoln Center for the Performing Arts Library; Metromedia Productions, David Hellerman, *Stereo-Review*, Sidney Skolsky, *The Fort Worth Star-Telegram*, John Lissour, Herb Helman, RCA Records; the BBC, Henry Brief, Recording Industry Association of America; *Newsday*, *TV Guide*, A.P., U.P.I., Captain Peter Hefler, Pentagon, Wash., D.C., Bill Stein, NBC-TV Publicity.

Contents

CHAPTER 1 NICE GUYS CAN FINISH FIRST

WE LOVE JOHN — FAR OUT
A hand-lettered sign

Show time. Fourteen thousand people are watching home movies. Not pop art, or fancy odd nervous jangly shapes seen at many rock multi-media concerts. On giant screens they see peaceful blue lakes, rugged mountains, wildflowers, tiny streams and soft dreamy white clouds. Campfires. Animals romping free. A figure walking quietly in the woods. It is nature photography at its most beautiful.

Backstage, a young man, holding a guitar, waits to go on. He is all charged up. Cue: A voice comes over the mike. "Ladies and gentlemen, John Denver!"

John Denver, RCA record artist, jumps up, and goes on stage. Green-dotted flash cubes pop. He is wearing cowboy boots, a flower-print shirt, a blue denim suit with a belt adorned by a big silver buckle. And gold-rimmed glasses. On his wrist there's a mod Pulsar digital watch.

He's the guy walking in the woods—the pop

Thoreau. His hair is neatly combed and natural. He looks as genuine as whole wheat bread. He smiles as if he's happy to be there. It is a typical big night for John Denver.

Millions go to his concerts. Not long ago, for example, John gave three sold-out concerts in a row at Madison Square Garden. That's about 60,000 people in three days. And millions buy his RCA records and cassettes. And they watch him on ABC-TV specials and hear his voice in Disney movies ("The Bears and I"). And they see him on talk shows ("The Johnny Carson Show"). Quite a few have even seen him do a bit of acting on NBC's "McCloud."

In 1975 everything came up roses for John in the hotly competitive pop music business. The singer-songwriter won top honors in many of the polls conducted by the music trade papers (*Cash Box, Billboard*). *Record World* chose him as "No. 1 Singles Artist" and "No. 1 Male Singles Artist."

And down in Nashville, Grand Ol' Opry country, the Country Music Association named him "Entertainer of the year," while picking John's "Back Home Again" as "Song of the Year." John got the happy news while he was touring Australia.

In February 1976, CBS put on a TV special based on a People's Choice Poll. The poll found that John Denver was America's No. 1 popular music performer.

It is hard to imagine just ten years ago, he appeared on "The Merv Griffin Show" a nobody. In February 1976 Merv had a special ninety minute *salute* to John Denver and his music. He called him "a young man who is an institution in the business ... who's been enormously successful with a string of hit records and compositions. His songs are not only very beautiful and tremendously popular, but they have something to communicate." What's more, Griffin said, "You wouldn't want to know a nicer human being."

Denver, described by many in the music business as "a super giant in today's pop," is boyishly good-looking. Son of a former lieutenant colonel in the U.S. Air Force, he stands a little under six feet—five feet eleven inches. His weight stays around 145-150. He has good teeth, friendly brown eyes, and an ovalish face and collar-length blond hair. He resembles a friendly college instructor who will always take the time to talk to you.

Once John suffered from stage fright. Now he loves to be out there performing. The crowds, the lights, the chance of "sharing his music with people" gives him a high as does the rich oxygen air of Colorado where he lives.

His real name is Henry John Deutschendorf Jr. At thirty-two, he acts like a grown-up flower child. He sings about the beauty of nature, love, the joy of being alive. That's supposed to be old-fashioned. But not to John. His songs are mostly upbeat and generally autobiographical.

But unlike many "flower children," he is realistic, industrious, practical. Having been in the pop marketplace since 1964, he knows about booking problems and sound-system failures. He also knows that some regard him as a commodity to sell. But he doesn't let problems or negative vibes bring him down.

To Denver, everything that's happened to him since he turned solo in 1969 is "far out." But actually *he* isn't "far out." Fans like him because he appears real, not phony. He's not like the rock stars who wear eyeshadow such as Alice Cooper, David Bowie and Mick Jagger. Nor does he resort to ear-splitting superamped banks of amplifiers to get his message across.

He sings gently, quietly, even when he sings against militarism and war.

A few years ago, the singer-songwriter was at the Bitter End, a Greenwich Village night club in New York City. Smiling his impish smile that curls up in the corners of his mouth, he told about being on the road with his back-up group, Fat City, in 1971. On the car radio, he heard a cut from his lp, *Poems, Prayers and Promises*—"Take Me Home, Country Roads." Denver asked the driver to pull over to the side of the road. There he listened to the record through to the end. It was a magic moment. "It was the first time I realized I was a star!"

With increasing popularity, John has turned into a personality too. He's been written up in almost every type of publication, including *Time, Newsweek, Parade, Seventeen*, and *TV Guide*. And *The Rolling Stone* ran a fine taped interview titled, "His Rocky Mountain Highness." Even the library reference book, *Current Biography*, has a piece on him.

John Denver songs—"Back Home Again," "Farewell Andromeda," "Thank God I'm A Country Boy" are often quoted in school graduation exercises. Denver lyrics are also being used in homework compositions. It seems that his songs are weaving their way into the youth culture like those of the Beatles and Bob Dylan.

"The Tom Sawyer of Rock"—that's what *Time* called him—has also inspired swimmers. Recently, a seventeen-year-old New Zealand long distance swimmer, Lynn Cox, listened to John Denver songs to soothe her in long hours in the icy water, particularly "Sunshine On My Shoulder."

A Long Island policeman, Ben Huggard from Freeport, New York, listened to John's music on a grueling 162-mile thirty-hour swim from the Florida

Keys to Cat Cay in the Bahamas. I contacted Huggard. He told me Denver tapes were played on a lead boat that accompanied him.

I asked him, "Why Denver?"

The swimming cop answered: "John is my favorite singer, and I appreciate his love and respect for the great outdoors. Also it's the kind of music I felt I could respond to rhythmically."

To have become so popular, John works hard, very hard, but loves it. In 1975, for example, he once gave thirty-nine concerts in thirty-eight days. That's hardly a soft cushy life. Unlike some record names who operate as studio musicians, huddled over tapes and singing into mikes, John's schedule is heavy on travel and live performances.

He gets a big buzz out of being in front of people and performing. Often without a real dinner, just a burger and a Coke, he'll go out, and do a show full of high-octane energy and good humor.

Sometimes his mother and father see John perform. John's mother cries. "They are happy tears," he says.

As a concert performer, John is redhot as a pizza oven. He's considered one of the "superstars" of the multi-billion personal appearance business. He has packed them in everywhere: sports arenas, concert halls, campus auditoriums, and convention centers.

Everywhere he plays, John draws "dream crowds." Some rock groups, by their material and on-stage tactics, draw audiences that somehow get into fights, break seats. It's gotten so that some promoters are putting into their contract clauses that the performers will have to pay damages. John Denver doesn't have to worry about that. His audiences are well-behaved. They come to listen, not to fight. There's no doubt that John Denver is hooked into peace-loving middle-America.

When he first started out as a solo artist, it was just John, his guitars and a truck. That's all. Today, it's more of a John Denver travelling show. Usually, he works two to four concerts a week, and he works on a percentage basis. They say he makes $10,000 profit on a concert. That's left over after paying off a music director, travelling musicians, sound men, light men, special security. Upwards of thirty people are employed in a Denver concert.

In small, intimate-type concerts John just uses a small combo backing (usually bass, fiddle, and banjo). On occasion he hires a backup singing group. And sometimes, he works with a big twenty-four-piece orchestra.

On the road he reads, he plays chess with his back-up musicians, writes songs, keeps in touch with his manager, Jerry Weintraub of Management III in California. John is also a fan of a brand of psychology called *est* (Erhard Seminars Training). And he's mighty fond of his special breakfast: ice cream (yes, ice cream), orange juice, a raw egg, plus a protein supplement that's supposed to be good for everything, hair, skin, circulation, energy, all whirred up in a blender.

A reporter who traveled with him was amazed by his politeness. He says, "Yes, sir," and "Thank you," to cab drivers, waiters, motel maids, doormen, studio janitors, security guards, lightmen. John explains it's nothing much. "I was brought up that way."

Not that John doesn't use a curse word now and then—he's not that pure. Mostly, he's friendly and low-key, not acting the Big Star. John wears informal clothes most of the time, some of it off the pipe rack. For TV he sometimes wears handsomely tailored and expensive shirts and slacks.

Through the years, he's worn a medallion around

his neck, "War is hazardous to children and other living things." Before it was mostly a thought. Now it's more personal since he and his wife Ann have an adopted son, Zachary (adopted as an eleven-month-old baby), who is now about two years old. John's home is Aspen, Colorado.

On stage and on TV and at recording studios, he wears glasses. Gold-rimmed, round-lensed glasses. Which brings me to this true story. A West Coast social worker was working with a teen-ager, very shy with girls, generally insecure. He wore black-framed glasses. One day a girl told him he looked "like John Denver."

He said, "Really?"

She said, "Yes. You do."

The boy glowed. He went out and bought himself new $45 glasses, gold-rimmed. The social worker said: "It did him a world of good. It did tremendous things for his ego."

John, of course, is known for his gold-rimmed glasses, while many pop figures who can't see five feet ahead of them put on contact lenses. John wears glasses because he has to. In fact, right after high school when he thought of becoming a military pilot like his Dad, he couldn't make the United States Air Force Academy due to his nearsightedness. Otherwise he's in excellent health. He claims he hasn't had a cold in years.

Denver sings in a light, pleasant tenor in the medium range. His voice matches his material. Gentle and reedy. It's not a powerhouse tenor. It's an easy-going voice, not gritty or harsh. He sings lyrics clearly. He doesn't have a regional Southern accent. And his arrangements, worked out mostly with the aid of his musical director, Milt Okun, fit the Denver vocal chords.

This largely self-taught singer-songwriter-guitarist has built his success on his own, despite the critics. A few have given him good notices. But others have tossed darts at him for being too bland, too simple, too cheerful. Recently one pop music writer wrote, "He's so nice, in fact, that people have said that watching him is as exciting as baby sitting for your younger brother." A *Village Voice* critic called him a "comic strip hero." Sharp words. Unflattering comments. But it hasn't stopped pop music fans from going to his concerts, watching him on TV, and buying his records. And ticket sales, TV ratings and record receipts are the name of the game in pop.

England too is Denver country according to *Variety* in April 1976, John "sold out a week's concerts at the London Palladium in one day."

In the business, his record sales are considered fantastic. Since 1971, he has been hitting the best-seller charts consistently. Five years of steady and ever-increasing popularity shows that John Denver has staying power. Gold records, platinum records, few returns, all suggest solid market support. John Denver has truly become the top folk singer in America.

CHAPTER 2 GROWING UP—AIR FORCE STYLE

"I was a lonely kid," John Denver says. "I never had close friends because just when I would acquire them, Dad would yank me out of school because we were moving again, to Alabama, or Arkansas, or some such place."

Like sons and daughters of many military families, John had a special kind of childhood: nomadic, gypsy-like. He was always moving, always having to adjust to new places, new faces. He was always having to tell kids, "So long" or "Goodbye." John's father, a career officer in the U.S. Air Force, a pilot, was constantly being transferred from one air base to another.

The rangy singer-songwriter was born in sun-kissed Roswell, New Mexico, December 31, 1943. New Year's Eve. Right at a time when World War II was at its blazing fury. Roswell was far away from the European and Pacific battle fronts but it was in the "thick" of the war. The cotton farmers near Roswell were busy growing fluffy white cotton, raw material for uniforms and bandages as well as clothes for the civilians. And the big cattle ranches in the Pecos Valley were supplying beef to the war effort at home and abroad.

John's father (friends called him "Dutch") worked out of the big Walker Air Base. The Walker Base buzzed with activity—green student pilots taking lessons, planes coming in and going out, taking off, practicing attack and evade tactics. In a cockpit, in the wild blue yonder, the young Oklahoman was becoming one of America's most skilled military pilots.

When John was born, his father was twenty-two; his mother, nineteen years old. Henry Deutschendorf Sr. came from Corn, Oklahoma, a rural town. Mrs. Deutschendorf, the former Erma Swope, is a native of Tulsa. John's father, a husky six footer, enlisted in the Air Force in 1940.

During the war, and after, young Deutschendorf Jr. had to live wherever his father was sent: Oklahoma, Texas, Alabama, even Japan. It was a constant round of new bedrooms, new PX's, packing and unpacking, flying, driving to new homes. It may be that the hectic traveling was a plus in the long run for John Denver. As a pop singer, he had to move around quickly to do one-nighters, and his travel experience made it easier for him to accept the constant change. Later, this wandering inspired his first hit song, "Leaving On A Jet Plane."

In 1949, when John was six years old, his mother gave birth to another boy, Ronald. (Today, Ronald is a sturdy, well-built twenty-seven-year-old movie photographer; he resembles a rock singer with shades and mustache.)

Though the Deutschendorf family was expanding, the military atmosphere was the same—overpowering. By the time John was two, World War II was over, but soon came the Korean conflict followed by the birth of the Cold War. The youngster with the brown eyes saw life as one air base. He'd played with a lot of kids from other service families. Mostly he saw a blur of tan-khaki Air Force uniforms and braided hats.

His father's career was upward and onward. First he was a pilot with prop-planes. Later in the 1950's in the jet era, his father became an outstanding jet pilot.

In 1961, he set a world speed record with the Hustler, a supersonic B-58 bomber—1200 miles an hour. John's father holds three records for military aviation. (The Air Force says a military record in aviation is a "first" in some areas such as going the highest in a certain aircraft, or the fastest.)

As John moved from babyhood to boyhood his features took definite shape. He was getting to look more like his smallish mother (a woman with a catchy smile). However, in his size and tallness, he looked like his father, a handsome rugged man.

John changed schools as often as a TV repairman replaces transistors. He remembers the lighter side of grade school. "It so happens I'm a marble freak," John mused in recalling his elementary years to a reporter from *The Saturday Evening Post*. "There was always some kid in class who'd stick them in the sockets of his eyes."

Then something happened that changed his life. In the seventh grade, his grandmother gave him a 1910 Gibson acoustic guitar. "It was a guitar she had played as a young lady," he says. John took instruction on it for a year. But he got bored with the chord exercises, the fingering, the sight-reading and dropped the lessons. Despite this, "Music got to be an important part of my life," he says.

Besides music, John also discovered segregation. Traveling around the country he found that schools were different in different parts of the country:

"That's a traumatic period when you're going through a lot of change. At the time we were moving from Arizona to Alabama; it was hard. I didn't know or understand anything about life in the South. For the first time there was a problem of color.

"In Arizona, you went to class with Mexicans, Negroes, whatever. In Alabama, you were only going with white kids in school. I was aware of differences, social political, racial, but I never thought about them. I don't think I had a point of view. I just absorbed things for a long time."

In Alabama, thirteen-year-old Henry Deutschendorf Jr. started school not knowing a single person. Then he got into chorus class. The teacher asked: "Why are you taking chorus instead of study hall?"

John replied, "I like music and I play guitar." The teacher asked him to bring his guitar to class. Soon John got to know a lot of kids. People said "hello." "I got to be known as a person—more than one of the service brats coming through (Maxwell Air Force Base) each year," he says.

In the late 1950s, the rolling stone of an army family came to a halt in Fort Worth, Texas. A former general, Dwight Eisenhower was President and a young Congressman from Massachusetts, John Kennedy, was organizing a run for the Presidency. Young Henry Deutschendorf Jr., the future John Denver, entered Arlington Heights High School.

Of Fort Worth, John once said, "That was the last place I lived before I left home and went out on my own. They had military people coming in and going out all the time, and nobody cared about you. You might make friends, you might not. I used to sing in church choirs and I joined the boys' chorus. Through a little form you filled out, they found out I played guitar. They asked me to bring it to class. I sang a song I had written and all of a sudden people were saying hello to me and inviting me to parties."

The guitar paved the way, but John's easy grin and good nature made friends for him, too. A *Rolling Stone* reporter, Chet Flippo, who talked to former Arlington Heights classmates in Fort Worth, said they referred to John as a "nice guy." Some called him "Mr. Nice Guy."

After school, John worked. He got a job at McCrory's Five and Dime on Camp Bowie Boulevard washing dishes, making the minimum, seventy-five cents an hour. Cleaning the grease-smudged burger plates and the frosted milk shake glasses wasn't glamorous but John could use the money for personal expenses and records. By this time, his playing and singing was good enough for him to join pop/rock groups and perform at local affairs.

John also played a little football, but mostly his life revolved around school, his job, music, and church fellowship socials. About those days, John told *Seventeen:* "Being a teen-ager, that's a hard time in anybody's life. More is expected of you. You want to get your act together because you want to grow up and want your life to mean something. So the first responsibility is to be honest within yourself."

Despite his winning personality, John was shy with girls. "I was very shy," he said recently on "The Merv Griffin Show." "When I was dating, I didn't date much. In high school I dated three or four times in three years. That's ludicrous."

Denver seemed to be an average student. In art he did show an aptitude for drawing and design.

As John's playing improved, Denver's parents bought him an electric guitar with its own little amp. He got into singing ballads that were on the charts. He also did some country-flavored Everly Brothers songs. When he graduated, his folks gave him, as a graduation present, an expensive Fender Jazzmaster

Pro Amp. In local groups around Fort Worth, he played lead guitar on the Fender and he played it smoothly.

In the late 1950s, the pop music scene was changing (it always is). Rock'n'roll was pushing hard against Tin Pan Alley, jazz and show music. Perry Como, Frank Sinatra, Andy Williams were still singing the skillfully crafted pop ballads. But Elvis Presley was slowly capturing the youth market with his mix of country music and black rhythm and blues.

Another big trend was the way folk music was making it in the pop marketplace. Folk music suggested the people, and the roots of America, an unslick kind of homemade music.

Those were the years John's musical tastes were being shaped. A new generation of folk singers were around, not "the originals" such as Woody Guthrie, Josh White and Leadbelly. This was a new generation of folk singers. Unshow biz, they wore slacks, open shirts, moccasins. The natural look. Mostly, they came out of the colleges and the coffee houses. They sang traditional folk classics, but also new songs fashioned out of current events. One group that affected John Denver deeply was The Kingston Trio. They recorded for Capitol, and they had a fabulous streak of best-sellers including "Tom Dooley" and "Lemon Tree."

But John wasn't listening only to the Kingston Trio. He also was listening to rhythm and blues (Jimmy Reed), the Ventures (an instrumental-type group built around guitars), Elvis Presley, and a boyish All-American singing group, the Chad Mitchell Trio.

To a great extent, John's present-day musical style and choice of subject matter reflect what he listened to on records and radio in high school. He has a fondness for folk music, a desire to use folk music forms with new contemporary lyrics, an openness to rock and country music. He also dresses in a folk style. While he doesn't wear the neatly pressed slacks and open-shirt costume of the 1950 college days, he sticks to unshow biz clothes, jeans, boots and mod shirts.

John's senior year at Arlington Heights High School was painful. He'd cracked through and made many friends. But his music-making brought him into direct head-on conflict with his parents. When his guitar playing started to take time away from school, chores such as cutting the grass, or working on the family car, there was tension and blow-ups.

Then, too, the family was fearful of John getting too hooked on music as a career. The Deutschendorfs enjoyed movies and watching TV. But they thought that show business people led crazy lives full of wild carousing and drinking. Also, according to John, "Music, always the thing I loved best, wasn't considered any way to make a living."

The arguments got hotter in the Deutschendorf household. John decided to act.

"I ran away when I was a senior in high school," he told *Rolling Stone*.

John took off for California, hoping to get a job. But soon his money ran out. The teen-ager phoned his parents. His father went to the West Coast and brought him home.

What should he do with his life? How should he earn a living? "The only acceptable thing I seemed to enjoy was drawing and designing. So I thought a bit and decided 'I'll major in architecture.'"

Tally Ho! John Denver goes fox hunting in England—in a cowboy outfit. *(Photo Trends)*

Enjoying the outdoors back home. *(RCA)*   Printed in U.S.A.

John Denver horseback riding without a horse. (Photo Trends)

John Denver singing "Rhymes and Reasons" with folksinger, Mary Travers. (BBC)

Going it solo on the coffee house circuit. *(RCA)*

John Denver guest - stars on the NBC television show, "McCloud." *(NBC)*

Hug me, I'm John Denver. *(RCA)*

John Denver at his triumphant homecoming concert in Fort Worth. *(Fort Worth Star Telegram)*

Performing on British television. *(BBC)*

Guess who is hosting the Johnny Carson show? *(NBC)*

CHAPTER 3   COLLEGE MAN

There followed the whole nervous bit.

Something almost every American college-bound high school student and family goes through: finding the right college. Reading the college catalogues with thousands of confusing facts about degrees offered, student life, teaching staff, student financial aid. Friends' suggestions are checked out. There's a lot of figuring out at the dinner table regarding costs, tuition, meal plans.

John and his parents picked Texas Technological College, in Lubbock, in the western part of the Lone Star State. Now it's known as Texas Tech. They had heard good reports about it. Slanted toward science, it was a college that intended to become a Southwest M.I.T.

Mr. and Mrs. Deutschendorf heard that the engineering department was very good. And they heard that the architectural department was under the watchful eye of the college of engineering.

At nineteen, John arrived in Lubbock in August 1962. With him were his clothes and his precious guitars and his amp.

His hair was short, almost a crew cut. A photograph in the college yearbook, *La Ventana,* of that year shows him wearing a dark suit, white shirt and slim tie. And he was smiling that broad, toothy, John Denver smile.

Of those days John says, "If I grew up to be an architect my dad would be pretty happy with me. My folks paid my tuition, room and board, and I earned the rest."

John found the college experience "awfully exciting." It was a youthful world in itself. The campus was so big (1,839 acres) it took time to learn your way around. It had countless buildings.

Although Texas Tech had fewer students when John went, it now has an enrollment of more than 20,-000 with a superb new computerized library, new medical center, University Center for concerts, and a new arts and architectural complex. Among the specialties besides engineering, are textile studies, petroleum research (many Tech graduates are in the oil business) and arid land development.

The architect-to-be soon discovered that Texas Tech was rah-rah-rah about sports, particularly football and basketball. The athletes were called Red Raiders. (Today you can buy Red Raider license plates frames, Red Raider T-shirts, Red Raider drinking glasses.) The town of Lubbock itself wasn't too small or too big, about 160,000 population. It was a quiet, conservative, religious-minded town, about 320 miles west of Dallas.

Denver enjoyed architecture. He worked long hours hunched over his drafting table with pen, pencil, and eraser. He started to look at buildings with a new eye. He spent a good deal of money on supplies. He got to know how to use architectural drafting equipment and supplies: the special inking pens, the cutting tools for models, T-squares, tracing paper, mat knives, illustration board.

He built models and heard about great U.S. architects such as Louis Sullivan, Frank Lloyd Wright, Philip Johnson, and I. M. Pei. He also was taught about basic structural engineering, how to build buildings that would withstand tornadoes and windstorms that cause so much damage in the Southwest.

John's courses weren't a snap. I know a little of what John went through. My son, Joshua, is a second year architectural student at Cornell. He loves architecture. He finds it exciting. But it's hard work, with many "all nighters." Designs and models take a lot of time. Often students doze off at their drafting tables. The lights are on all night in the architectural drafting rooms. Sometimes the students (lots of girls too) have six hours of sleep in a three-day period.

When John entered Texas Tech, a young blue-eyed president was in the White House, John F. Kennedy. He was talking about full employment and rebuilding the slums. He spoke of establishing a Peace Corps in which young Americans would go abroad and help poor people develop their talents and their resources. From time to time he spoke of a faraway country called Vietnam; he was sending military "observers" over there.

But John wasn't too interested in politics. He was just interested in making his way, taking his courses, and making music. A friendly, gregarious, people-oriented guy, John joined a fraternity, Delta Tau Delta. Some friends called him "Dutch," his father's old nickname.

Soon he started to perform in frats and in joints along "The Strip." The social life at Tech centered on the fraternities and sororities—and The Strip, a half-mile long stretch of restaurants, beer and pizza places, bars and coffee houses outside the city limits.

John spent a lot of time singing and entertaining

with a folk group, The Alpine Trio. He also worked with a rhythm and blues combo, The Caravans, and he gave as many solo performances as he could fit into his schedule.

He found himself drifting into the life of a campus musician. At Tech he grew more skilled, more proficient with the guitar, more self-confident as an entertainer. He was comfortable entertaining college students. He was like the youthful coffeehouse-type audience. He understood them, dressed like them, and could kid around with them in their own language.

Compared to his studies, the immediacy of the pop world was tempting. A building takes a long time to design, process through the building department, longer to finance and build. In pop music you sing a three minute song and if the audience likes you—Instant Applause. Pow!

"People were willing to listen to me and singing for them was the only way I got high," he says.

Though tall and on the thin side, he also played a little football with his frat brothers.

In an interview with *Rolling Stone,* he said: "All of a sudden I was on my own. Didn't have to go to bed at any particular time, could study when I wanted to —and my grades showed it—and I really enjoyed playing football. It was a very carefree time.

"I was majoring in architecture, which is something that I really enjoy. But a lot of stuff I was doing just didn't have any meaning for me."

He got deeper and deeper into music. He was picking up the vibrations from records and things he heard on the radio: the works of Tom Paxton, Joan Baez, Peter, Paul and Mary, the New Christy Minstrels and the Chad Mitchell Trio.

It was the early 60s, and the folk boom was at its

height. New writers like Phil Ochs, Tom Paxton, and Bob Dylan were emerging. They called themselves contemporary folk writers and they wrote topical songs, protest songs, children's songs. And the arrangements were often modern with fresh harmonies prepared by skilled arrangers. A man named Milt Okun acted as musical director for many Peter, Paul and Mary albums and Chad Mitchell albums, too. (Later Okun was to be John Denver's musical director.)

Inside easy-going Denver, a conflict was blowing like a Texas windstorm. He was very fond of architecture. But he seemed to enjoy making music more. And he knew you couldn't be an architect and a professional musician at the same time. There are many fine architects, doctors, lawyers, social workers who are excellent amateur part-time musicians. But pop performing as a career demands concentration. It takes all your time getting around, performing, planning, going "on the road."

In his mind, John was wondering what he ought to do. But he wasn't prepared to leave school yet. He stuck it out at Tech.

Summers he worked to make money for living expenses. One summer he worked in the wheatfields of the Midwest. Another summer, at the end of his sophomore year, he got a job in the Pacific Northwest in a logging camp in the state of Washington. The loggers called him "Tex." He sang at night, played the guitar. They were a hard, tough lot. John liked them, and he played and sang and they enjoyed him. But once, on a July 4th, he got his guitar smashed by one lumberworker who didn't like a Hank Williams song he sang.

In the fall of 1964 the pressure began to build up once again in John to try for a career in pop music. "During my junior year," he says, "the grades began to suffer, and I decided to drop out and either get the music out of my system or see what I could do with it."

Young Deutschendorf Jr.'s decision wasn't easy to make. His parents, friends, classmates in the small architectural department, were shocked. But the Southwest folk-rock Hamlet was doing badly at school. He couldn't concentrate on sketches and structural analysis while he was thinking of new songs, learning new lyrics, chord runs, strums, listening to the latest hits on the radio and performing. He wanted to be in the thick of music, not on the margins. He wanted to be a full-time professional guitarist and singer.

John's plan was modest and level-headed. He wanted to drop out for a single semester and try his luck in California. He wanted a six-month shot at show business to see if he could connect. He had saved up $125.

He talked it over with friends in his frat. Then he wrote a letter to his parents about wanting to leave school. He gave them the reasons why. Luckily, he had the most understanding mother and father. Henry and Erma didn't agree with him. They thought the decision to leave school was crazy. In another few years he would acquire a Bachelor of Architecture and be set professionally. But John stuck by his decision.

John praises his parents' role during this difficult time. "My decision must have been a real heartbreaker for my folks, but they were beautiful about it," he once told *The Denver Post*. "They gave me $250 they had put aside for my tuition and told me to go do what I had to do. They said, 'We don't approve but we'll always help you. If you get into trouble, call."

"That's the best thing parents can do for a kid—give

him the space to try what he wants. A lot of people think love means hanging on to somebody saying 'Don't leave. I need you.'

"But that isn't love. Letting someone go, that's love.

"You know I've never acknowledged to myself what my folks did for me until recently. I was meditating before a concert, just letting my mind float and that dropping out of school incident came into my head. To my parents at that time, music must have seemed like the worst—it took me away from my studies to strange places with creepy people. But they helped me."

John couldn't sleep for a week. Got his things together, packed and said "Goodbye" to friends. It was rough. Nobody said an encouraging word.

"When I left college there was not one person, my friends at school, instructors, there was no one who said, 'Yes, you should go forth,'" John says. "Everybody thought I was making the biggest mistake of my life."

CHAPTER 4   FAREWELL LUBBOCK, HELLO CALIFORNIA

In 1964, after two and a half years of college, John drove off the Texas Tech campus in an old '53 Chevy with $375, his clothes, and his three guitars. With every passing mile, he felt freer and lighter. He felt that he had made the right decision.

To John, Los Angeles probably seemed to be a natural place to go. He had been there before when he ran away as a high school student. The sunny pleasant climate also matched that of Lubbock.

Going to the West Coast turned out to be one of the smartest moves he ever made. It brought him self-confidence and contacts. And in pop, as well as anything else, contacts are 80% of the game.

By the 1960s, pop was taking on a sun-kissed California color. More and more hit recordings were being produced there. And every type of music could be heard: show songs, Frank Sinatra pop, contemporary-pop (Beach Boys), country, and rock. In 1964, a West Coast-based company, Capitol, was riding high with nine Beatles' gold records.

Beatlemania, Presley-rock, and Hollywood musicals were cutting into the folk boom which started with the Kingston Trio in the early 60s. But contemporary

33

folk was still alive and kicking. Up and down the West Coast, there were still perking coffee houses and filled folk clubs such as San Francisco's *hungry i*. And there were still hootenanies, where practically everybody who had a guitar and knew a chorus of "John Henry" could go on stage and sing.

Through a friend of the family, a civil engineer who lived in Long Beach, California, John got a job as a draftsman.

Nights and weekends, he knocked on doors, looking for a gig. He sang in "hoots." One of his first jobs was as a warm-up man in a popular night club. He managed to hold the attention of the audience who were waiting to hear the "main acts." John Denver entertained under the name of John Deutschendorf.

In *Rolling Stone,* John gave the details of those early days in Los Angeles. "I went to all the hootenanies and they were going on everywhere in L.A. The second year I was there I went to Ledbetter's which was owned by Randy Sparks." (Note: Randy Sparks was an early folk impresario, songwriter and founder of the popular New Christy Minstrels, a big chorus-sized folk music group).

"I sang and he came back after the show and said he'd really liked my voice, and would like to talk to me about working there."

(Now John recalls that somebody made a tape of those days, and he was really "bad.")

A Capital Records executive saw John perform and persuaded him to make a "demo." Later the suggestion was made that John change his name.

"A big heavy meeting was held and somebody said, 'Listen, kid, Deutschendorf has got to go.' I felt badly about that, but I also felt that I wasn't going to allow that detail to come between me and what I wanted to do with my music," says Denver.

So John settled on "Denver" because it brought up the image of "mountains." Also, he says, "I guess he thought Deutschendorf wouldn't fit on a record label."

About the "demo." Nothing happened. Capitol chose not to use him as a record artist. In pop music there is one law: Don't believe you have a record until it is recorded, pressed and *in the stores*.

Dream sequence. Looking back, John recently remembered how he dreamed of being a pop star. "I was sitting on a lifeguard tower and aching to sing to people," he told *TV Guide*. "I dreamed about it. I wanted to do what I felt I could do, do it so well that there would be more people than we could handle. And I can tell you how hard I dreamed. I dreamed just hard enough to make it real and now it is."

Anyway, he worked at Ledbetter's for fifty-six weeks. Later he got a job in Phoenix in a club, the Lumber-Mill.

In 1965 he heard through the folk grapevine that agents were looking for a replacement for Chad Mitchell of the Chad Mitchell Trio. Mike Kirkwood of the Brothers Four, who had seen Denver perform, recommended him to Milt Okun, arranger and music director of the Mitchell Trio. John grabbed a plane to New York where auditions were being held. It was a very jangly, competitive scene. An army of folk musicians was there, strumming and fretting.

It would be great if John got the job. He used to listen to their records, and he liked them. They were one of the first early, clean-cut folk pop groups, along with the Kingston Trio. They sang old songs and new contemporary songs, even folk-flavored songs from Broadway musicals. They recorded for Mercury.

Besides those who turned up to audition live, there were about 200 tapes sent in.

The Chad Mitchell Group was a hit group and an

interesting one. The trio started singing together in 1959 at Gonazga University in the State of Washington (where Bing Crosby went to school and sang with bands). A Catholic priest got them together. Chad Mitchell was the son of an Oregon shipyard worker, Mike Kobluk, a Canadian, came from British Columbia. He started singing in a high school glee club, knew Gregorian chants, and was of Ukranian descent. Joe Frazier from Lebanon, Pennsylvania, was the son of a steel welder. In high school he studied voice.

In a preface to the *Chad Mitchell Songbook,* Robert Shelton wrote that they were "one of the ablest singing groups." They were also "commentators who were willing to speak out and sing about the stupidities, foibles and prejudices they see around them."

Anyway, guitar in hand—and with a bad cold—John auditioned. The job open was to replace Chad Mitchell who had decided to quit.

I contacted Chad Mitchell in late December 1975. He was on the comeback trail as a solo singer-performer in the Ballroom in Soho, New York City. He told me that he had decided to leave because he was tired of the "road." He also thought he was getting "too old" to appear at colleges. Also, he felt that the heavy rock and the Beatles would put them out of business "within a year."

"I didn't audition him," said Chad Mitchell. "Joe Frazier and Mike (Kobluk) did. I didn't know who John Denver was. Neither did they."

The story goes that Denver at first imitated Chad Mitchell—one of his idols. Frazier and Kobluk weren't happy with that. They asked him to be himself, sing his own way, not to copy.

Joe Frazier and Kobluk liked what they heard, and hired him as lead-singer and guitarist. The cheerful, tall, easy-going tenor was on his way. Incidentally, neither of the other two played an instrument. The trio was renamed the Mitchell Trio.

So, in 1965, at the age of twenty-two, John Denver, now his show business name, became a full-time member of an established pop group. Before he could catch his breath, he was on the road, a grueling, frantic sort of life. He moved from city to city by plane, bus, or car on split-second schedules.

"One of our first concerts together was back at Texas Tech," John recently recalled in the alumni magazine, *Texas Techsan.* "When I came back to the campus, everyone was saying, 'Hey, Dutch, see ya tonight,' and sure enough, the auditorium was packed. Half of them must have been fraternity friends, and other people who had heard me in Lubbock.

"I was so scared I couldn't even remember my name. It must have been the worst performance of my life."

As a member of the Mitchell Trio, he sang songs by Phil Ochs, Bob Dylan, the Beatles (Lennon-McCartney). Also the Mitchell repertoire included the satiric "The John Birch Society" and gospel songs "I Feel So Good," a stinging number about education, "What Did You Learn In School Today?". There was also a funny one called "Super Skier" by Bob Gibson. It's a funny-sad song about a skier who never skis (a "sundeck Charlie" who watches girls and other skiers). But somehow he is talked into going on the slopes and he is demolished, colliding into a tree. The moral of the song is "for girl watchers and boywatchers": don't let anybody lure you onto the slopes.

John also wrote a few songs which the trio recorded. "For Bobbi" and "Like To Deal With The Ladies." And on the record labels and jackets he used his real name, H. J. Deutschendorf, Jr. His parents got a kick out of that when they saw those records.

John blended into the group nicely. His voice worked well with Mike's and Joe's. And he also added the backing of his guitar. From his apprenticeship days with the trio, John learned a lot. Professionalism. He worked day in and day out in front of audiences, sharpening his delivery, his singing, his guitar-playing.

He started to write. He got to know show business. Lots of hard work, particularly when you're on the road. The Mitchell Trio was a performing group; they relied on concerts and personal appearances to make money—and to sell records. They weren't a studio group that just made albums. But luckily John was tough inside.

He had worked as a paper boy, had worked in dime stores; had worked summers when he went to college in lumber camps and wheatfields. It was rough but John could take it. All he needed now was a special person with whom he could fall in love.

CHAPTER 5   ANNIE

In November 1965, the Mitchell Trio (Mike, Joe and John) played a college date at Gustavus Adolphus College in St. Peter, Minnesota. Just another gig. Nothing special.

It's a small college with about 2,000 students. Adolphus was founded in 1832. A handful of students come from foreign countries (Asia, Africa), many from Minnesota and surrounding states. Adolphus is run and owned by the Lutheran Church. The town where the college is located is small, population around 9,000. It's seventy miles from the twin-cities of St. Paul-Minneapolis.

Just another college date. But it was to change John's life and even inspire him to write one of his most popular love songs "Annie's Song."

It so happened that the Mitchell Trio was set to perform during Community Chest Week, a week-long series of events to raise money for worthy charities. And during this week, John met a pretty blue-eyed five foot two inch brunette from St. Peter, a co-ed named Ann Martell.

It turned out to be an off-again on-again romance. John told what happened to Olga Curtis on *The Denver Post*.

39

"We did our concert and then the students did their show, and one skit had this girl who came up with signs like 'Act One' 'Act Two' 'Applause.' She was wearing jeans and a red shirt and had beautiful dark wavy hair, and she looked so alive. That caught me. I fell in love with her right then.

"But I couldn't figure out how to meet her. I'm shy with women unless it's business. I kept hanging around and pretty soon some students asked me to sing, and then she joined the group. Well, I sang every song to her.

"I told her who I was. Later I sent her a Christmas card with my name and address on it. She didn't answer. About a year later in October 1966, we were doing a concert in Minneapolis, and we had to drive through St. Peter to get there. I'd never forgotten about Annie and I was telling one of the other guys about her and he was impressed. Man, imagine remembering one girl for a whole year!

"He got her phone number for me from some girl student. I called and said, 'You won't remember me. I'm John Denver. Do you want to come to my concert?' When she said 'yes,' I think I drove eighteen miles to her sorority house in eighteen minutes.

"Two nights later I invited her to another concert fifty miles away and she came, and I was hooked. I had it so bad I flew to St. Peter between concerts and when bad weather grounded all the planes, I took a train to see her for a day.

"Just before Christmas of 1966, I was in Los Angeles and the Trio was having trouble, and I was homesick and lovesick. So I called her and invited myself over to her house for Christmas. That's when I found out she was going to a place called Aspen the following month with her college ski club. I decided to tag along."

Once there, John went crazy about the beauty of Aspen. He told himself that when he had money, this is where he wanted to live and settle down. With Annie, of course.

Back on the bus to Minnesota, John proposed. She said, "No." He told her that he wouldn't ask again unless he was certain the answer was "Yes." John didn't phone for a month and then a friend of hers called to tell John that Annie was lonely. He raced to the phone and proposed once more. Annie said "Yes."

The wedding, a church wedding, took place June 9, 1967 in St. Peter, Minnesota. The bride wore a white lace gown with a chiffony veil. John wore (would you believe?) a cutaway tux, vest, Ascot tie, and flower in his lapel. He resembled an All-American boy with a crewcut, and a grin you can see in a million wedding photographs. He says he hasn't worn a suit since.

But things didn't proceed happily ever after. He says they had "a horrible first year."

Impractical, John hadn't thought of where they were to live, or what Annie would do while he was scuffling on the pop circuit. At first they lived in Edina, Minnesota. Then they moved to a little apartment in Chicago. (Mercury, the company for which the Mitchell Trio recorded, was headquartered in Chicago.

The smiling bride and the smiling bridegroom were troubled. The trio (Mike, Joe and John) was coming apart at the seams. The Denvers didn't have too much money. There was precious little sunshine around. He didn't have the bread to take Annie along. So the young bride was left alone in Chicago, not knowing anybody.

"Man we had a lot of fights. It's amazing we ever got through the first year," John says.

There was a lot of infighting and bad feelings

41

among the Mitchell Trio, too. Joe was getting interested in rock. He thought the trio ought to go with rock. Mike and John fought the idea. They wanted to keep to folk and topical music. Joe Frazier, perhaps out of unhappiness, started to miss rehearsals. He showed up late for rehearsals, and once he missed a concert in New England. That did it. There were angry words. Joe departed (some say he was "fired"). That left Mike and John holding the fort. Things were in a bad way.

Meanwhile, the pop scene was mixed up in 1968. No single trend dominated. Rock was very strong. Yet hits were being cut by a wide variety of performers and groups: Elvis Presley, The Rascals, The Monkees, Bob Dylan, Otis Redding, the Doors, the Turtles, Ray Charles, Herb Alpert and the Tijuana Brass, and Dionne Warwick with the Bacharach-David tunes.

But the contemporary folk groups as represented by the Mitchell Trio were on the decline. Bookings were harder to come by, audiences were slimmer, and record sales merely a vinyl trickle.

"That was the period," John says, "when folk music was becoming a dirty word. Folk music is supposed to be the music of the people, and to express their feelings. There was a war going on, and a lot of performers were pretty outspoken against it."

The Vietnam war bitterness, poor bookings, personal tensions had an impact on John and Mike. They had words. John was especially unhappy and angry. Things couldn't go on that way. Finally Mike and John had a big blow-up. Mike decided to leave. By that time, the Mitchell trio was $40,000 in debt. John promised to continue the Mitchell Trio and pay back the money owed.

John continued with the Mitchell Trio name for

awhile, assisted by David Boise and Mike Johnson. They he dropped the name, and just had a trio called Denver, Boise and Johnson. It, too, folded—with $11,000 in debt.

CHAPTER 6   GOING IT ALONE

Confused, troubled, not knowing what to do next, John decided to go to Aspen to think things out. Figure out a new direction for his career.

He remembered Aspen, Colorado. He had loved it there when he went along with Annie and her ski club before they were married. He would rest and recuperate from the break-up of the Mitchell Trio and his own group.

John was in his middle twenties, twenty-six, and married. He was at a turning point in his life as a singer-songwriter-guitarist. In the business, he was a slight "name." A former member of a respectable performing group, but so were countless others who were formerly with the Moonshiners or the Highwaymen or the Tarriers or the Limelighters.

Aspen. Eight thousand feet above sea level. When he got there the picture postcard town lifted his spirits. It was as pretty as he recalled, in Central Colorado, a beautiful spot, with a population of under 2000. It was once a silver mining center. Now instead of miners' picks and sturdy miners' workclothes you saw skis, bright-colored ski clothes and in the summer, Bermuda shorts and musical instruments.

Mostly, Aspen is a little Camelot, filled with

streams, rolling hills, wildflowers, blue skies and snow-capped mountains. People discovered it, and turned it into a year-round resort. Businessmen came there for conferences, but it's also a center of musical activity—folk, jazz, classical.

The town takes pride in one of the country's best classical music festivals, The Aspen Music Festival. Hundreds of students come there to study, learn and be coached by great classical artists such as violinist Isaac Stern (he played the opening theme in the movie version of "Fiddler On The Roof").

On long walks, John Denver thought hard on what he should do next.

Should he organize a group under his own name? Or should he go solo? And if he went solo, could he make it? With a group there's less performance pressure. There's people to help you out in case you don't feel well one night, or if you're low in energy. When you're solo, facing the audience alone, there's no one to depend on but yourself, night after night.

He decided to go it alone.

The rangy singer-songwriter got himself a one-week job (at a low salary) at The Leather Jug, a ski lodge at Snow Mass, near Aspen. There he started to sing evenings when the skiers returned from the lifts and the ski slopes. There they'd sit around while fireplaces roared, and they would listen to Denver sing.

John worked easily before this crowd. It was a youthful atmosphere, similar to college audiences. People liked the cheerful, easy-going performer, his unaffected smiling face, his little jokes to the audience, his imitations of a trombone.

He stayed there for a month. But John knew if he was to get anywhere he couldn't hide in a ski lodge. He loved Aspen, but he had to work elsewhere, and get around if he was to make a dent in the pop music business. He had to move on. In show business you've got to go where the audiences are, particularly if you aren't an established star.

Often he'd get on the phone and book himself for concerts and folk night club jobs. These were rough days for John. He did everything for himself but usher. He recently recalled one of those concerts in *Stereo-Review*.

"I remember very well going to Cedar Rapids, Iowa, making all the arrangements myself, getting there when it was ten below zero and having to load these five boxes of sound equipment on a truck and drive to the gym. I'd left my gloves home, this time I'm thinking about, and it took me about twelve minutes to get this darn thing up and into the truck.

"Drove over to the school, got some people to help me unload, took a shower, got tuned up and all and did a two and a half hour show."

During this period, when he got a job in a Washington, D.C. folk club, The Cellar Door, he met two people who have figured prominently in his career—Bill Danoff and Taffy Nivert.

At the time, Danoff was functioning as a sound and light man at The Cellar Door, but he was also a performer, a member of several groups that played in and around Washington, D.C. When a member of his group left, Taffy joined. A pretty blonde, she was twenty-six years old then, and a typist at the AFL-CIO national headquarters.

Bill was an interesting guy, a graduate of Georgetown University where he majored in Chinese. Taffy had spent two years at Steubenville College. Bill played guitar and Taffy played the tambourine and kazoo, and both wrote and sang. John and the two of them hit it off, and soon they were writing with and backing John Denver.

Later they formed Fat City. Their name goes back to an old folk expression which means "easy street." They've played together off and on since 1968. Together with John, they wrote quite a few songs including the million-seller, "Take Me Home, Country Roads." It was to be a most important association for all of them.

Back to Denver's bumpy road to fame. John continued to play anything he could book—high schools, coffee houses, colleges. After campus concerts, he slept in a dorm; mornings he ate in the college cafeteria. He was slowly building his name. His manager, Jerry Weintraub, told *TV Guide* about this stage of John's career.

"He was out singing his songs to the people. John wasn't selling any records and being out there was the only way he could get his message across. It was like a grassroots campaign. We went to the people first, and the people said, 'You're great, John.' John was selling out in Texas, Iowa, St. Louis, and Kansas City before anybody in New York knew who he was."

In 1969, John Denver became nationally known. He had written a song called, "Leaving On A Jet Plane." Peter, Paul and Mary liked it and recorded. It became a million seller and a No. 1 song on the charts. Not only that, Liza Minnelli and Andy Williams recorded it. And United Airlines used it as the basis of popular TV commercials. John made himself quite a bit of gold with the song.

Soon he was being billed as the writer of "Leaving On A Jet Plane." Naturally, he got more bookings, plus some good reviews. Also, he was starting to define himself as a performer and as a songwriter. He was moving toward songs, contemporary in feeling but folk and country in style, that emphasized his inner feelings and the goodness of life. By being autobiographical he found he could be true to himself. He hit a responsive chord in others, too.

In mid-69, Denver's career spurted ahead. RCA gave him an audition, liked what it heard and signed him. John's first record was a single, "Rhymes and Reasons." In October 1969 John's first album was put out with the same title, *Rhymes and Reasons.* Having records out gave him national exposure over the radio.

There followed other lp's, *Take Me To Tomorrow* and *Whose Garden Was This?* in 1970. Fair-sellers. But in 1971, a Denver single from his lp, *Poems, Prayers, Promises* burned up the charts—"Take Me Home, Country Roads." A New York nurse, who drove cross-country that year, says, "Wherever you went, you heard one song, and that was 'Take Me Home.' I became a John Denver fan."

The hit record resulted in more profitable concert dates. Let's focus on one at the huge Greek Theatre in Los Angeles in 1972. In the concert program John was described this way:

A composer with a heartful of soothing sounds, a sensation with his first song, "Leaving On A Jetplane" and continuing with his latest, "Aerie," making an even greater impact with his new music.

John came backstage about 8 P.M. for the 8:30 concert wearing casual clothes. If he wore a tie, his fans would probably kill him. For this particular concert the Denver production people were experimenting with a technique other artists were using— multi-media. They set up projectors to flash on slides while John sang. However, during the concert, the slides didn't work too smoothly. But it didn't seem to bother the audience, consisting mostly of young people, from sixteen to the mid-twenties.

Also on the bill were Fat City and Dick Gregory, the comic-activist.

John got fine notices. *The Los Angeles Times* praised the "pleasant appealing show." *The Los Angeles Herald-Examiner*'s music critic wrote: "Denver is another of the seemingly endless crop of composers who turn out quality songs. He's also a superior guitarist and has a delightful voice. . . . His greatest asset talent, however, is an open-faced honesty and a wide-eyed enjoyment of the people and the things around him. . . . He seemed genuinely amazed and happy that he was appearing on the stage of the famous Greek Theatre and that people had actually paid to see him."

John did his usual mix of songs like "Leaving On A Jet Plane," "Aerie," "Sunshine On My Shoulder," and "A Train Called City Of New Orleans."

The show ended on almost a poetical note. The audience and cast joined in singing "America The Beautiful." It was a beautiful moment.

In 1972 he continued to build his popularity. He and his manager, Jerry Weintraub, decided John should be more visible, and do more TV. Except for guest shots here and there, John hadn't worked TV much. The decision was that John start in Great Britain. He did a guest shot on a program hosted by the American song-writer-singer, Tom Paxton, titled "In Concert." John knew Paxton, sang his songs, and the show came off quite well.

A BBC producer, Stanley Dorfman, who saw him remarked "Wow! Let's give him six weeks." (Memos went out to schedule a Denver series.)

Meanwhile, John did other guest shots. He appeared on "Sounds For Sunday" and on that program he sang his standbys, along with new songs, "The Eagle and the Hawk" and "Goodbye Again," both written with guitarist Mike Taylor. He also did "Carolina On My Mind," by James Taylor (one of his favorite songs) and a children's song, "Butterfly." The BBC reports that it was with "Tom Paxton's powerful (anti-war) 'Jimmy Newman' that he had the studio audience on its feet and cheering."

In 1972 John also did some U.S. TV including some guest shots on "The Johnny Carson Show." He also participated in an ABC-TV program designed to get young voters to register and vote in the Presidential elections—"The Midnight Special."

In 1973 John Denver returned to Great Britain and guested on the show, "They Sold A Million," because "Leaving On A Jetplane" sold a million. Then the BBC-2 announced that it was giving him his own series. "The John Denver Show" premiered on Sunday, April 29, 1973. With him were his friends Taffy and Bill.

John tried not to let the strain of putting on a TV series bother him.

"I'm consciously working at not taking myself too seriously," he said. "I'm not important and I don't want to be. I'm not making a message with my music. I'm simply expressing myself in the avenue that's open to me."

John liked the TV scene especially for giving him the opportunity to meet other artists. "When I'm in the States I'm doing concerts and I don't get to see anybody," he told *The Rolling Stone*. "I'd love to spend time with Carly, James, Joni, Elton, the Beatles—I learn from them. Just before Christmas I got the new LP's by Carly (Simon), James (Taylor) and Joni (Mitchell). They were so good. . . . I recorded my own version of 'Fire And Rain,' but I can't think of a better way to do 'One Morning In May' than James Taylor did."

When he finished the BBC specials, John returned to the U.S.—and to continuing steamheat popularity. 1974 was another heavy year for John. He played top-grossing concerts; the booking agents couldn't get enough of John Denver. And he had a couple of important gold records: The Recording Industry Association of America announced two John Denver million-sellers: the single, "Sunshine On My Shoulder" and the album, *Back Home Again.*

One particularly sweet touch of success stands out in 1974.

That's when John Denver returned to Fort Worth where he had lived as a teen-ager to give a concert. The papers gave it a lot of play as did the disc jockeys. The place: the giant Tarrant County Convention Center. The date: a Friday night in October 1974.

The Fort Worth Telegram Star referred to him as one of that city's "most famous ex-residents." Many of John's classmates and lunchroom acquaintances were there, kids he met at church socials and at high school. Of course they weren't teen-agers any more, some were married. Tickets were hard to get for that concert. For John Denver wasn't little Henry Deutschendorf, Jr., but a national pop star. He was on RCA records, could be heard on the radio, seen on TV, and his name was on those little white tabs in juke boxes.

When he appeared on stage, John smiled his sunny smile and said he "waited a long time" to return to the city. He kidded about the Tarrant County Convention Center, describing it as big enough to be a "small plane depository."

The concert itself was a smash, a glowing happy

home-town triumph. John even did a little juggling with three oranges, but he dropped a few.

Performance, a hard-nosed publication put out for those who book acts into concert halls, reported, "John Denver's eagerly-awaited homecoming concert drew the largest response for tickets since Elvis Presley's last visit."

In all this, Denver was proving to himself and the music business that he wasn't one of those flashy hyped-up one-record artists. He was an artist with staying power. He was a singer-songwriter whose name kept turning up on the charts. Not a product of gimmicky electronics, but a concert performer with personality.

Those days of doubt, the blue-days when he first turned solo in that Aspen ski lodge, The Leather Jug, seemed far away. In six years he had gone very far, farther than he had dreamed.

He had decided to go solo—and had succeeded.

He had met and signed with a brainy and enterprising manager, Jerry Weintraub.

He had radio and TV exposure, both at home and abroad.

He had several million selling singles and lp's on RCA.

He had developed a musical personality of his own.

CHAPTER 7   JOHN DENVER, STAR

1974 was a very good year for John Denver. But 1975 was a fantastic year.

Concerts: In that year, the singer-songwriter-juggler was one of the biggest money-makers. Bookers of auditoriums and arenas who gamble thousands of dollars with every name they select, couldn't wait to get Denver's name on a contract. During a recession when audiences were watching every penny, Denver was selling out.

Variety wrote in its year-end 70th anniversary issue: "In 1975 most of the superstars, John Denver, Frank Sinatra, Rolling Stones, et al continued to do the smash business expected of them."

Get that? Expected of them. That's praise indeed.

Records: Sales of his records (and when we use the word records we also mean 8-track tapes and cassettes) were tremendous. Some music people credit Presley and John Denver for helping put RCA in the black, after a period of weak sales. Fans were picking John Denver material from the nation's display racks and the record bins at a hot and heavy pace.

Even Mercury Records tried to cash in on the Denver craze. It released a package containing sides previously cut by the Mitchell Trio with John Denver.

The artwork played his name very large:

BEGINNINGS
JOHN DENVER
with the
Mitchell Trio

In 1975, Denver had three singles million sellers and two Gold Record albums. They were "Back Home Again" (single), "Thank God I'm A Country Boy" (single), "I'm Sorry" (single), *An Evening With John Denver*, and *Windsong*.

Special Engagement: John also did something novel in 1975—he played Lake Tahoe, Nevada. There in one of the oddest double-bookings, he was co-starred with Ol' Blue Eyes—Frank Sinatra—back to back, on the same bill for seven nights at Harrah's. More than 670,000 persons tried for reservations. Only 14,000 could see the show.

Apparently, nightclub types didn't hold John's sunny wholesomeness against him. John got on the floor without the slick production or chorus girls, did a show and got excellent reception. Probably more than he or his manager figured on. It was taking a chance putting John in the nightclub atmosphere (the image, you know), but it didn't seem to bruise Denver, or hurt his standing among his fans.

Harrah's turned handsprings with joy. It took an ad in *Variety*:

"Throughout the years, Harrah's has always meant the biggest names in show business. 1975 is no exception. As a matter of fact we were the scene of the greatest event in nightclub history . . . the Denver/Sinatra 'Back to Back' Show."

TV: The story is boringly similar—success. John put on an ABC-Special, "An Evening With John Denver." What happened? The National Academy of Television Arts and Sciences gave him an "Emmy."

Polls: Each year, the music business trade papers—*Cash Box, Record World, Billboard*—pick the "tops in pops." They go over masses of information, run through thousands of figures, check airplay in various regions of the country, talk to record retailers and wholesalers and rack jobbers (who handle department stores and supermarkets). It's pop music's own popularity contest.

Pop figures and groups and their managers and relatives and wives worry about these polls. High ratings on these polls mean more TV engagements, publicity, and increased fees for personal appearances.

In the Male Vocalist category, *Billboard* chose as most popular John Denver and Elton John—something unusual, a tie.

In another category, Best Artists of 1975 on Albums, John Denver placed second, next to Elton John, also one of the hottest names in popular music.

In the *Cash Box* poll, the Top Pop Singles Vocalists picked were John Denver and Elton John, again a tie. And in another category, Top Male Vocalists, Elton John placed first, and John Denver second.

Record World picked him as No. 1 Singles Artist and No. 1 Male Vocalist.

Special Award: Country music, a big hunk of pop, has a Country Music Association (CMA). Every year it gives awards—its own kind of "Oscar." Down in Nashville there's a dinner and reception, and countless country stars and groups gather to hear who the country music artists, managers, songwriters, and record executives pick as winners.

John wasn't present. In October 1975 he was touring in Australia giving concerts. But in the country down under he heard the happy news that he was chosen "Country Music Entertaineer Of The Year."

Not only that, his song, "Back Home Again" was chosen as "Best Song."

As John Denver would put it, "Far-Out."

CHAPTER 8   CLOSE-UP

In pop music circles, promoters are hunting for singers they can make "John Denver types"—clean-cut, friendly, and warm pop performers. But, of course, John is not something artificially put together by PR image makers. He's an individual with his own flavor, somebody people respond to. One fan puts it this way, "He's real." *Newsday*, a New York newspaper, agrees. "Despite his success he has remained as unaffected and pure as the mountain springs that flow through the Rockies of his beloved Colorado." Folk singer Tom Paxton adds, "There's no artifice to John."

But let's look more closely. What kind of person is John Denver really?

Although a pop millionaire, John hasn't lost his common touch. He prefers campfire cookery to fancy gourmet restaurants. The lush greenery of the Rocky Mountains pleases him more than the emeralds you can buy at Cartier's. When he goes on tour, he stays at ordinary motels.

Like every pop music personality, he is shaped by the pressures that exist—concerts, recording dates, TV specials. Yet he has managed to keep his balance, to keep things from getting flaky. His boyish good spirits shine through off-stage and on. John himself says,

"I'm no different off-stage than I am on-stage. Because you can't come to my show without laughing with me and laughing at me, and having fun. And that doesn't happen at a Rolling Stones concert."

However, John can react sharply, too. He can be hurt. Of a bad review, he once told a reporter, "I ask you, was that an article or an editorial?"

The close relationship of pop performers with their audiences pleases him. "Young people understand rock musicians, who they feel are friends. We are the spokesmen for our generation. If someone thinks, when listening to me, well he sounds like a nice guy, or somebody I want to know, then maybe he will tune into my particular lifestyle. Non-violent. Non-aggressive. Very gentle."

Everybody knows him as John Denver. Yet, John says, "I've never legally changed it (his name). I'm still John Henry Deutschendorf, Jr. and I'm also known as John Denver, and both are O.K. with me. I'm proud of both."

Denver has a great respect for people who work for a living. As noted before, he is polite to motel employees, bus drivers, sound-men. Sometimes, he does more than smile pleasantly. Not long ago, when he and Frank Sinatra co-starred back to back in Harrah's in Lake Tahoe, the entire engagement was sold out quickly. So John and Frank did a special show for the employees who couldn't get tickets. It took place at 3 A.M.—only for the employees—and nobody had to pay to get in.

About politics, John Denver seems to be divided. Once he expressed an interest in *Rolling Stone* on running for office. But he also says, "I don't think that politics right now is something that's working. I personally think that my music is working better than politics in regard to serving people." It's not clear whether he will support any of the candidates in the '76 elections. If he does, he probably will support a liberal. In 1972, he did a little song-campaigning for Senator McGovern in his race against President Richard Nixon.

In another interview, with *The Saturday Evening Post,* he sort of downgraded political activity that goes on in state legislatures and in Washington, D.C. "People on an individual basis will make changes, not protesters—or lobbyists. People who do what they really know to be right or true. Little things. In traffic, in grocery stores, you let somebody else in front of you. That's peace."

While John believes in fun and a relaxed way of looking at life, he also is a tremendous worker. "My music" is uppermost in his mind. He rarely cancels an engagement or commitment. He isn't one of those "no show" pop personalities who cross up fans and concert bookers by showing up late or missing a performance.

These days, he is asked to speak and sing and lend his name and reputation to hundreds of causes. Denver and every other show business personality are fair-game to politicians and fund-raisers. When you have a big name at a charity auction, benefit, or rally, you can build up the audience and raise more money. So Denver picks and chooses carefully which events he will attend. Often he'll appear without a buildup—and for free—at an elementary school. Not long ago, he gave a benefit for a paralyzed cheerleader at the University of Minnesota.

An active type, John likes to do things—make music, sing, ski, go camping, go horseback riding, play golf. He isn't the sit-on-the-sidelines spectator in an easy chair watching the world go by. When he bought a horse to ride, he told *Newsday:* "I have been riding horses ever since I could get on a horse. But I never owned one till now. The *Windsong* album cover was taken in California. I made arrangements to get a horse on the beach at dawn. I was riding and racing with the wind."

Of course he is most proud not of his horse, or his house in Colorado, but of his new son, Zachary. "Zachary is the best thing that ever happened to me," he says. He's such a happy father that he has written a song, a sweetly sentimental ballad, "A Baby Like You." He wrote it for his son and for Angelina, the granddaughter of his friend, Frank Sinatra.

John is very much against drugs. Once he told *Time:* "If people want to get stoned and tripped out on acid or Jesus, that's their business. But if things don't work out, I've got something else that will: love, appreciation and sincerity."

His anti-drug stand and his clean All-American image received a jolt not long ago. On a tour to Australia there appeared a story in which John was quoted as saying that he had used marijuana. But John replied that he was misquoted by the sensation-hungry Australian papers. He explained to *Newsday:* "I was taken out of context at this so-called press party or press conference, or whatever you call it. There is no truth to it."

John firmly believes you can control your destiny. "I try not to waste too much time and energy on negative things, so that I can get everything out of what is. Like I tell my audiences before each show. I would like them to relax, enjoy themselves and go where the music takes them."

A host of psychologists (from behaviorists to Norman Vincent Peale to Dale Carnegie) believe in the power of positive thinking, too. This technique is important to John. He also thinks you dream in a positive manner, fantasize happy visions, they may come true. "If your pictures are wonderful, then your life is gonna be wonderful." He adds, "If I can create strong enough fantasies for all those people through my songs, or whatever, then perhaps they'll direct their lives toward some of those good feelings."

Some may challenge this as much too simple. The individual may have a happy frame of mind, but problems can be so sharp, in regard to jobs, family problems, friends, discrimination, corrupt politics that happiness is blocked off. But sour vibes do not do you any good either. A positive attitude can't hurt.

There have been rumors that John has been into Transcendental Meditation and encounter groups, but John has denied this. However, he has become an enthusiastic devotee of a San Franciscan, Werner Erhard, founder of a brand of psychology called *est*. That stands for Erhard Seminars Training.

The pop star first met Erhard in Aspen. In the beginning, he frowned on the man's ideas and methods. Then he came to see them as a tool for self-improvement. John claims that he's learned a great deal how to meet problems and cope with society as it is via *est*. "It's enhanced by awareness," he says. "It's the most interesting thing I ever came across since I can remember and it had a great bearing on my life."

There are some interesting aspects to *est*. One technique of consciousness-raising used by Erhard consists of people sitting on chairs (or lying on the floor) from 9 A.M. to 4 A.M.—a nineteen-hour stretch. A "course" consists of 60 hours, over three weekends.

Erhard is a controversial figure. More than 75,000 people, including Valerie Harper, Yoko Ono and Joanne Woodward have taken his training courses which are usually held in hotel ballrooms and cost $250.

Some psychiatrists and social workers feel that Erhard is a kind of slick medicine man, an authoritarian figure who practices Instant Therapy. One former *est* student, writing in the *Village Voice*, wrote a piece saying it has some good insights, but she "saw people take *est* and become like robots." (For additional material on Erhard you can read Adam Smith's *Powers of the Mind* and *est* by Adelaide Bry).

It is an odd coincidence that John Denver's parents now actually live in Denver. They're not too far from Aspen, where John makes his home. Though retired from the U.S. Air Force, John's father, Lt. Colonel Henry Deutschendorf Sr., isn't really retired. He has taught pilots to fly corporate planes for busy executives. And now he occasionally flies John to concerts in a Lear jet. When they have a little free time, John and his father play golf together.

John's mother, Erma, works as a hospital volunteer. She also spends time on a giant John Denver scrapbook.

The Deutschendorfs are famous on the street where they live because people keep saying: "Oh, you're John's parents? Well, what's John really like?" Naturally, they are very proud of their son.

Denver believes in himself, too, but he also knows the value of others. He relies a lot on the judgment of his personal manager, Jerry Weintraub, who guides John's career. Weintraub, a New Yorker, now spends a good deal of time in California. *Billboard* has described Jerry as a "mighty manager." He saw possibilities in John in the days when Denver was just struggling along.

Besides John, Weintraub represents many other artists. He handles Charles Aznavour, the French singer-songwriter, for U.S. projects. He also helped produce *Nashville*, a stinging film that touched on country music, political manipulation and violence. His wife is Jane Morgan, a pop singer, famous in the 1960s. Weintraub is also known as an expert tour packager for Frank Sinatra and Elvis Presley, as well as for Denver.

John and Jerry produce their own TV specials. Their TV production company is called, fittingly, John-Jer Productions.

Another name worth noting in the John Denver success story is Milt Okun, a former New York vocal music teacher fascinated by folk music and opera. He's the singer's musical director, acting as arranger and record producer. Okun is also an executive of Cherry Lane Music, which puts out Denver's songs. On the side, when he has some free time, Milt edits music books. He put together the best-seller, *Great Songs of the Sixties*, published by the *New York Times*. (John was represented in that anthology, by "Leaving On A Jet Plane.")

Recently, John, Jerry and Milt went a step further—they established a new record company—Windsong Records. Launching of Windsong follows a pattern set by a flock of other record stars. The Rolling Stones and the Grateful Dead have production firms of their own, so does the Jefferson Airplane (Grunt Records) and Elton John. The Beatles were among the first of the hit groups to form their own company, Apple Corps.

John will continue to record for RCA Records which will manufacture and distribute Windsong products. Among those who have already cut discs on the new label have been Fat City, Taffy Nivert and Bill Danoff. They're in a group called the Starland Vocal Band.

John, of course, is happy at his economic success, the money keeps rolling in. (He claims he doesn't know how much money he has.) But he is equally happy for the joy his music has given to others.

In 1973, CBS put on a made-for-TV film, *Sunshine*. It was a moving feature based on a true story of a young woman's battle against terminal cancer. As she got weaker and weaker, she found comfort in listening to Denver's music. Her last request was that his song, "Take Me Home, Country Roads" be played at her funeral.

After a concert, many pop stars and groups race backstage where they are guarded with maximum security: private guards with walkie talkies patrol the corridors and hallways leading to the dressing rooms. The fans cannot approach the stars. It's O.K. for the public to buy tickets and scream approval but not to get too close to the great ones.

There is private security that guards John Denver backstage after a concert, too. Normal type security, to keep order. But John isn't standoffish, and fans are often allowed to approach him.

And after concerts, people will come up to him and talk about what's happening in the world, about how they feel, about causes to be promoted, or protests that should be made. John sometimes disagrees with his fans over method or strategy. But he listens.

Those who go to his concerts and buy his records look on the laughing, bespectacled guitarist-singer not only as a pop star who's up there on the charts and on the TV screen. To them he is a friend, somebody they can talk to and relate to.

And that makes John very happy. As he puts it, "People can do things to widen the gulf between being a star and being anyone. What I want to do is narrow it."

CHAPTER 9 THE SUNSHINE KID:
IS JOHN TOO HAPPY?

"He is a seller of dreams." *TV Guide*
"Mr. Clean With Guitar" *Saturday Evening Post*
"He's as safe as pasteurized milk." Don Heckman,
New York Times

Despite the slings and arrows of critics and the fickle taste of the American public, John Denver is a pop force. Why is he so successful? What's he got that hundreds of other pop/rock/folk singers do not have? Three things stand out like a Colorado sunset.

1. In a world full of trouble John sings of sunny, happy things. To many fans, John represents a return to a simpler life, a return to nature. He sings of love, the love of a good woman, of children, of the rivers and the mountains.

He also sings of "roots"—the importance of a home. And he does songs about finding out who you are. While some of his songs are sad, mostly he sings of the joy of life and the possibilities for people to be happy and to grow. Millions identify with his inspiring message.

2. His own optimistic upbeat nature.

3. His skill as a singer-songwriter-performer makes

it all work. He packs his message in a neat vocal pack-
ages and ties it up with a touch of naturalness. He is
popular because of his ideas. But if he didn't have the
ability to write music and lyrics and perform them before large crowds, he would have turned into just another guitarist struggling to make a living.

O.K. With that as a framework, let's go take up
what the critics say. They charge, for example, that
John Denver is too sweet, too icky, too goody-goody,
too cheerful. They say he's a singer of sweet dreams
during a time of crisis, crime and corruption, not to
mention unemployment, racial strife and urban decay.

Is Denver too happy? Is he a maker of fantasies, an
escapist?

On stage, for example, John kids around, cracks
jokes. He beams like a sun-ray lamp. He does little
trombone solos with his hands. Or he juggles. (That
astounded a critic for *Billboard* reviewing John's first
Carnegie Hall concert in 1972.)

Denver is quite different from many pop stars who
are deadpan. Byb Dylan, for instance, looks sullen, almost lemon-sour when performing. That's his image,
serious, mad-at-the-world. There are rock groups who
are still into weird rock-theater, such as the Who. At
concerts, the Who, famed for *Tommy*, still break guitars and dropkick amplifiers.

Even that's pretty tame stuff nowadays. There's a
heavy rock group, Kiss, on Casablanca Records, which
uses smoke bombs, blow torches, sirens, rocket firing
guitars, and make-believe blood in its act. Another,
the Blue Oyster Cult, goes on stage in black leather,
along the lines of storm troopers.

John begs to differ. He's there to entertain, to
spread joy. Crazy theatrics that spotlight violence are
not his style. If he puts on slides it's not of "blood" or

psychedelic op art but of the beauty of nature—streams, flowers, winding roads.

Of course, John is aware of the seamy side of life. For a long time, John has done Jacques Brel's "Amsterdam" from the hit musical *Jacques Brel Is Alive And Well and Living In Paris.* The song tells of the rough and tumble world of sailors—the fights, the cheap beer, the lowdown honky tonks of Amsterdam, Holland. Hardly a cheerful song.

And John also sings songs by Tom Paxton that hit hard. One's called "Forest Lawn," about a Hollywood cemetery that is so commercial they sell souvenirs from the funeral store. Another is the anti-war ballad, "Jimmy Newman." This is interesting because John is the son of a Lt. Colonel of the Air Force (retired). And he's recorded "Whose Garden Was This?" another Paxton song about sci-fi and the future, an age in which people have never seen meadow or smelled flowers. We don't know why; perhaps an atomic war or pollution has killed all living plants.

In the John Denver songbook, there's also a surprising item, a protest song, "Wooden Indian," words and music by John himself. It has a powerful lyric, perceptive, poetic and strong, attacking the white men for taking over Indian lands, and telling how the land grab has hurt the Indians as a people. There's even a hint that one day the redman may rise. Bob Dylan couldn't have handled the theme any better.

So the charge that John Denver is a Johnny-one-note *only* singing about happy things isn't accurate.

Now let's take up the charge that John is The Sunshine Kid: that he's too cheerful. But John isn't a pioneer in happy songs. Contemporary pop, Broadway musicals, film musicals, jazz, folk music are packed with good feeling sunny songs. Songs full of the joy of being alive, of hope. Here are just a few with notes on who wrote them or recorded them, or shows they came from.

"Feelin' Groovy"	Paul Simon
"Cockeyed Optimist"	From "South Pacific"
"Singing In The Rain"	From MGM film of same name
"On The Sunny Side Of The Street"	Dorothy Fields/Jimmy Van Heusen
"Get Happy"	Harold Arlen/Ted Koehler
"Everything Is Beautiful"	Ray Stevens
"Ac-Cent-Tchu-ate the Positive"	Johnny Mercer
"Joy To The World"	Three Dog Night
"Why Can't We Be Friends?"	War

This doesn't mean that John Denver can't be criticized. Perhaps he is not angry enough. Perhaps he is so happy, successful and fulfilled that he fails to see perils around us sharply enough. But not every artist has to be angry. Not every record personality has to sing the blues. As John said in *Seventeen,* "My music is very positive and optimistic. If you look around today, there's not much pop music that fits that description. I think life is perfect, and basically, if you are in touch with yourself and life around you, no matter what you do and who you are, you can be very successful at living."

And a lot of people like what he has to say. One Minnesota pop observer wrote me: "People here are very into all the clean air, fresh water, country living type stuff, Minnesota's 10,000 lakes, etc. So folks identify with the values that J.D. espouses."

John Denver's songs have also done a lot for the

ecology movement. Wendy Pettigrew of the Sierra Club says: "Environmental songs are very influential in helping to change values and help in making us more understanding of what is going on around us."

Also, John keeps away from drug-stained lyrics. And he keeps away from "suggestive and risque" lyrics. There's been a lot of oversexed lyrics in pop, even in country music, with songs talking about "one night stands." The program director of WWVA in Wheeling, Va., recently reported that it is coming from rock musicians who want to pick up on the now-fashionable country music.

This program director told *Billboard:* "John Denver has proved that sensitive, clean and inspiring lyrics can become No. 1 in the charts, proving that nice guys can finish first."

Along with his songs, John, himself—as a personality—is upbeat. He makes people laugh, he kids around. That adds to his cheerful image. An ABC executive, Frank Brill, vice-president in charge of variety programs says: "John takes you somewhere sane, calm, nice. That's the effect he has on people. And it's not the music. It's *him.*"

The early days—John Denver with the Mitchell Trio. *(Mercury)*

Pop phenomenon John Denver accepting a gold record album with Milt Okun, Jerry Weintraub, and Frank Manici (l. to r.) *(RCA)*

Far out! (NBC)

Heading for the high country. (RCA)

(LA2) STATELINE, Nev., Aug. 6—SINATRA AND DENVER, BACK-TO-BACK—John Denver and Frank Sinatra are appearing this week at Harrah's Hotel-Casino in South Lake Tahoe, Nev., and more than 670,000 persons tried for reservations. Only 14,000 will see them in their seven-night stand. (AP)1975

John Denver and his beloved wife, Annie, on a Manhattan bus on their way to the premiere of *The Great Waldo Pepper.* (Wide World Photos)

John Denver poses with Mac Davis and Loretta Lynn in cere-
monies honoring John for best country album of 1974.
(Wide World Photos)

Who will soar the highest? John or his pet California Golden Eagle? *(UPI)*

John Denver at home. (RCA)

CHAPTER 10   HIS WORDS AND HIS MUSIC

"If you write in the folk/pop bag you gotta like John Denver."

The Songwriter

"A superstar songwriter."

ASCAP Today

John Denver's gold records, his songwriting awards, the sale of Denver sheet music points up the fact that he's definitely got a touch in the writing department. Let's begin this brief analysis of the Collected Works of John Denver (so far) with a brief comment by Mary Travers, a former member of Peter, Paul and Mary, and now a solo artist.

She told *Time:* "His songs are simple and hopeful. He is a very personal, conversational singer and he has a gee-whiz kind of humor which is refreshing."

His songwriting talent is worth analyzing. It's helped put him on top. His own homemade songs form the basis of his million-selling singles and albums, his tours, his TV specials. And they have a life of their own, too. He has a profitable and growing catalogue—more than seventy compositions already. They range from A-Z, from "Adagio" to "Zachary and Jennifer." He's written about prisoners ("Hard Life, Hard Times") and banks (a commercial titled "Sixty Seconds for a Bank").

One of the most popular songs by Denver is "Leaving On a Jet Plane" (Eighty records by various artists, so far, including the No. 1 click by Peter, Paul and Mary.)

Another smash is "Take Me Home, Country Roads" (Denver, Taffy Nivert, Bill Danoff wrote it together). Eighty-seven records, so far. Denver cut the big hit, of course, but it's also been recorded by Eddy Arnold,

What's John's songwriting personality? How does he write?

Olivia Newton-John, Loretta Lynn, Tennessee Ernie Ford, Ray Charles, Ferrante and Teicher, Henry Mancini, Wayne Newton, and Lawrence Welk. There's also been a European recording in French—"Mon Pays Est Ici." That's songwriting power, n'est-ce pas?

terribly complex, but is as direct as a spring rain shower. He rarely uses complicated chord changes,

His music is simple. It's easy to understand. It's not moving keys, novel harmonies, or irregular rhythms. Eight-track over-dubs is not his speed. Nor is the dense multi-layered polyrhythms of the hard rockers. He doesn't bombard your ears with bolts of sound. He prefers the route of gentle musical persuasion.

Basically Denver's melodies are folklike with a country flavor. (The arrangements, however, are often modern.) His tunes are soothing and hummable.

Denver has run counter to much of the current musical scene—hard rock, soul, disco-soul, and rhythm and blues. He is closer in feeling to Judy Collins, Joni

Mitchell and Gordon Lightfoot. Lately, however, there's been a return to melody in pop which Denver may have helped influence.

A few years ago it was different. *The Los Angeles Times* said: "Denver sees himself for what he is—out of place with the main-stream of current music. He was, after all, part of the late 50s, early 60s folkscene which included the Kingston Trio and Peter, Paul and Mary. If Denver is not a strong voice in the folk movement, at least he was one of its clearest."

Chad Mitchell thinks Denver is a bit of everything. "He's slightly down home, slightly country, slightly folk, slightly rock, slightly middle of the road."

His music works effectively to get his message across. A press release issued by Walt Disney Productions in connection with the film, "The Bears and I," for which John Denver wrote "Sweet Surrender," says "His songs hold a tenacious note of hope for the human condition, though Denver does not consider himself a great composer."

Great composer or not, John Denver has become a spectacular "cross-over artist." That's a music business term. It means that Denver isn't locked into any particular musical category. He is popular among contemporary pop fans, among those who are fond of folk music, those who like country music, and also those who are grooved into what radio stations call "middle of the road (MOR) easy listening."

Music is more than a collection of notes and chords. There's a feeling to tunes. His tunes may not be the most original to come down the pike, but there's a quiet gentleness in them. His sound isn't abrasive, raunchy or funky. And many people react to it favorably. It's music that sort of reflects a sunnier, happier, more easy-going frame of mind. And people like to listen to the calm melodies perhaps as a reaction against the nervous and uncertain world we live in.

"What I sing about is what I know," John says. "That's where the music comes from. I'm not trying to make life anything that isn't. What I'm trying to do is communicate what is so about my life, what I feel."

Denver's music has been both rapped and praised. One reviewer has called it "boring." Others say that he's the "Mickey Mouse of rock." But there are others who say pleasant things about his work. Mike Jahn, in *The New York Times*, once wrote, "In the realm of contemporary folksong, he rates quite high." John Rockwell, also of *The New York Times*, reviewing a Nassau (Long Island) Coliseum Concert, said, "The songs themselves strike some as simpleminded in their very simplicity, although at their best they achieve an evocative charm and lack of pretension."

Robert Hillburn of *The Los Angeles Times* says "Follow Me," one of his ballads, is: "One of the most successful love songs I've ever heard." The lyrics are O.K., the music better. The theme that bears the title is repeated three times, and is a graceful, well-constructed tune.

As to Denver's lyrics, they cover everything from love to "space" (a sort of climate in which to grow). He writes to make a point, not to create abstract imagery. His lyrics (sometimes he refers to them as "pictures") are usually upbeat, positive. Some of his lyrics rhyme, some are free and rambly ("Windsong"). He can also write a tight, compact story ballad such as "Two Shots." In "Sweet Surrender," a song he wrote for the pro-ecology Disney film, "The Bears and I," he refers to choices that people can make. We *can* change things. That's his message.

John's songs try to scale down our complicated world. A pop observer says: "It's accepted to be simple, to try to decomplicate your life. John Denver says that in his lyrics. People want to get back to the roots. The simple songs can be believed more."

Having once worked for the American Guild of Authors and Composers (AGAC), I am conscious of giving all the writers associated with John Denver proper credit. Besides Taffy Nivert, Bill Danoff and Joe Henry, he has collaborated with John Martin Sommers, Steve Weisberg, Laurie Kuehn, Michael Johnson, Dick Kniss, Mike Taylor, and others.

How difficult is it for John to get a tune in his head down on paper? Generally he starts with a phrase or expression he has heard or read. Sometimes a song begins with a chord progression he liked.

"I compose very casually," he told *The Denver Post*. "Things come into my mind when I'm sitting around the house, or when I'm tinkering with my acoustical guitars, or after a concert. I have to replace the strings on my guitars after nearly every show so there's a lot of thinking time."

Some composers write on fancy monogrammed musical manuscript. John puts down song-ideas on anything—paper napkins, motel stationery. Since he writes music slowly, he generally puts his ideas down on tape. Others work out the arrangements. John can't predict what song will be a hit. "With every song," he says, "there's a point where I'm sure it stinks." But of course, it rarely does.

John chooses subjects close to him. He wrote "Rocky Mountain High," about himself, life and Annie. He wrote "Aspenglow" because of his love for Aspen. Not long ago, he went on an expedition with Jacques Cousteau, The French underwater naturalist on *The Calypso*. Out of that John created a song, "Calypso," about the ship and the explorers who try to understand life beneath the sea.

How quickly does he write? It took him nine months to write "Rocky Mountain High." He got the idea on a camping trip he took at Williams Lake, outside of Aspen. He reports that he wrote "Annie's Song" in ten minutes on a ski-lift. He doesn't force creativity. He lets it come.

One of his numbers, "Mathew" came out of a real story. He just changed names. Sometimes others bring him a title or idea, and they work on it together, with John writing the music, or collaborating on the words.

Whatever methods he uses, John has had great success with music and lyrics. A New York music publisher told me with a sigh, "I wish I had his songs."

Denver's songs make a lot of money not only from record royalties and guitar book sales but from airplay as well. Everytime his music is played over radio or TV he gets paid through ASCAP, the American Society of Authors, Composers and Publishers, which collects monies from radio and TV stations.

In the ASCAP building in New York City, there's an Index Department which keeps files on songwriters and what they have written. In the files, you'll find the names of the heavyweights of American popular songwriting including comtemporary song writers such as Paul Simon, Carole King, Bob Dylan, Stevie Wonder, and Elton John.

There's a long song list that's expanding all the time under the name of John Denver. ASCAP considers him one of the very important newer songwriters. In *ASCAP Today*, its magazine, they are always running pictures of him and items regarding his awards and Gold Records.

If pop is a form of popularity sweepstakes, then clearly John has hit the jackpot. And one of the big reasons for it has been his songs and what they have to say. He says hopeful things, loving things, that people want to hear. His lyrics somehow provide warmth and understanding. He clues people into what to look for in life. Real lasting relationships rather than quickie plastic pleasures.

And he says it all with folklike melodies that are simple and tuneful.

CHAPTER 12 "ROCKY MOUNTAIN HIGH": FAMILY, SUN, BACKPACKING

Pop stars are forced to live in a closed-in world. Even John Denver. He has to spend a lot of his life in giant indoor arenas, concert halls, coffeeshops, motels, dull hotel rooms, airport terminals, backstage dressing rooms, recording and TV studios. Inside places, where there is tight security.

But when he has time off (and he makes sure he has time off) John Denver bolts like a colt to the wide open spaces, the un-nicotined air of his Colorado home. Specifically, Aspen. Birch-like Aspen trees are there with lovely greenish leaves that have sawtoothed edges. "This is the most beautiful place," he says.

Away from the pressures of performing, the hardworking singer unwinds. He loves the craggy mountains, the green grass in summer, the shiny white ski slopes of winter, the lakes. In that Rocky Mountain area (8000 feet above sea level) so high that the sun is brighter, the sound crisper, and the air cleaner, he finds peace with his wife, Annie, and their son, Zachary.

In 1975, he put some of his love for Aspen in an ABC-TV special, "Rocky Mountain Christmas." TV viewers saw John on horseback, skiing and clowning in the snow with Valerie Harper, star of "Rhoda." He also sang with Olivia Newton-John. Later John moved indoors into a see-through plastic dome. People sat around living-room style and John sang. In the distance you could see the snow-clad mountains. Perhaps a little showbusinessy, the TV special did capture John's sincere love for the outdoors.

John has even written a song about his favorite place, "Aspenglow."

Some pop stars who make it rent Hollywood movie star homes with swimming pools, and cabanas, six-car garages and twenty-eight guest rooms. John lives more simply. Not Poverty Row but in a modern three-bedroom $150,000 home. (The only really luxurious part is the land—seven acres). The former architectural student helped design the split-level structure that lets in a lot of sun and light. The Denver decor is mostly in warm earth tones: orange, green and gold, "It's the only real home I've ever had," John says.

Annie does a lot of the cooking, laundry, dusting. She's busier than ever since Zach's arrival. When John returns everything gets a little messed up. He is fond of a neat home. But when he comes home, he puts things away and then forgets where he put them. Not the complete liberated man, John doesn't do the dishes. However, he often clears away the table.

John likes Ann's cooking. She says, "He's a cook's delight. He eats like you wouldn't believe—huge meals in the evening. But I wish he'd eat more good breakfasts."

Besides being a homemaker, Ann is a fighter to protect the environment. In 1974 she worked as a volunteer in the campaign to elect Governor Richard Lamm of Colorado because of his ecology stands.

John helped, too, by giving two concerts which brought in $60,000 for Lamm and Senator Gary Hart.

In the days they are together, they are very much the married couple. They play catch-up in terms of seeing each other, seeing friends. They go to Aspen to the movies. John loves comedies.

The Denvers do not live alone. Hardly. Besides John, Annie and Zach, there are three cats (Alice, Harriet and Andromeda) and two dogs (Daisy, a gold retriever, and Murphy).

At home, John rests, thinks, listens to records, writes songs, plays with adopted son Zach. He loves ice cream (Baskin-Robbins) and Annie is always getting some from town.

About Ann, he loves her, and he says so proudly in print and to concert audiences. Once he was in Washington, D.C. giving a concert at the Capital Centre. He told the crowd there's nothing he loves more than performing—with the possible exception of Annie. Later in an interview with *The Washington Post* he went on to say, "Well, I really love this lady, and I don't think talking about her is an invasion of my privacy."

It may be embarrassing for Annie—this sort of disclosure—but John's not embarrassed by it. He likes to tell people how he feels.

In June, 1976, the Denvers celebrated their ninth wedding anniversary.

Annie doesn't usually go "on the road" with John. "My wife generally doesn't go with me," he says. "All my energy is directed in a specific area—that gets very boring for other people who have to sit around while we're out on the road."

Of course, Ann isn't glued to Aspen. She goes with John often to visit his family in Denver. And she accompanies him on special occasions. In 1975 she went with John to a Bnai Brith Dinner in Los Angeles where they honored his manager, Jerry Weintraub, as "Man of the Year." It was quite an affair. Among the celebrities were Wayne Rogers, formerly of TV's "Mash" and now starring in "The City Of Angels" and Richard Carpenter of the Carpenters. John performed. And she's also gone with John to the world premiere in Manhattan of the film, "The Great Waldo Pepper."

But there have been slight strains in the marriage. It's not easy being the wife of a pop star. John recently revealed on TV that there are all kinds of pressures because he's away from home so much. Annie understands him. But, he says: "It's been difficult.

"I love her as I love my music." To John, it's a matter of knowing how much his music means to him. "She accepts who I am." He added: "We support each other totally."

In the artwork of John's RCA albums (and on TV) the outdoors is stressed. One lp shows John riding horseback with an Indian headband across his head, and looking like something out of a mod dude ranch. But his fondness for the outdoors is real, not faked. He skis, golfs, rides horses. He also enjoys hiking in the surrounding Rocky Mountain countryside and going on camping trips with Annie and friends.

John also does a little do-it-yourself work around the house, and mows the lawn. His mowing technique is a little wild, as if he were Walt Whitman. "I have a handmower," he says, "and I like to go out on a sunny day when nobody is around, take all my clothes off and mow my yard.

"When I was growing up there weren't many yards, and I wasn't into working them anyway. But this. This is mine. My yard right there in the mountains, and I stand there naked and look around and think, *My God, I live here.*

"Blows my mind."

Denver guards his privacy, and the local papers seem to respect it. I checked with *The Aspen Times* and they said they rarely run any feature stories on him or publish any photographs of him with his family.

However, some visitors are really pushy. Occasionally people drive up the private road to his house and park and practically invite themselves in for coffee. Once a man drove up with a carload of people. Not only that, the car got a flat right in John's driveway.

"And I ended up helping him fix it," John said.

As a result, John has put up a sign that reads: "Please do not bother us. You are not welcome here."

Maybe the sign is a little harsh, but peace and privacy are what John came to Aspen for.

His days in Aspen follow a routine. He gets up early, about 7:30 A.M., has breakfast and feeds the Denver cats and dogs. Then he reads his fan mail. They say he reads all of it. However, a secretary answers the rather heavy correspondence. In that way, John keeps in touch with his fans.

Some mornings, when he's not on a backpacking trip, he goes over music, listens to records, plays with Zach. Often he confers on the phone with his manager, Jerry Weintraub, and his musical conductor and arranger, Milt Okun. Together they go over details of the John Denver hectic schedule which includes concerts, recordings and TV.

Nighttimes, he often probes the skies through a high-powered telescope. His interest in the planets and the stars finds its way into his songs ("Farewell Andromeda").

John sleeps in the raw. And sometimes he forgets to take his glasses off. Hollywood columnist Sidney Skolsky, who is an authority on what stars wear when they go to bed, got the bedside information from John himself.

Asleep, or awake, John prefers Aspen where it's quieter and more beautiful, than the big cities. However, he's not anti-big city all the way. He finds the noise and traffic "tiring." But he also admitted on "The Merv Griffin Show": "I enjoy coming to L.A. A lot of things I can do here I can't do in Colorado."

Nevertheless, those who prize the unspoiled wilderness find John in their corner. And his pro-ecology stance isn't all in his songs or his TV work. Not long ago he helped community people stop a road-building project through a beautiful part of the Rockies. John campaigned against it and got people to sign petitions.

John is also pressing RCA to use recycled paper in the packaging of records. Quite a few record manufacturers (Warner's, Capitol, Columbia) are into using recycled fibers in record and tape packaging, particularly lp sleeves and inner-record sleeves. Because of this change, thousands of trees will be saved from the chain-saw.

As to the future, John would like to keep on doing what he's been doing—writing songs, making records, putting on concerts, appearing on TV. He'd also like people to think of him as a complete all-around entertainer, not just a pop singer. He enjoys doing comedy and would like to do more of it. Movies, too, fascinate him. There was a rumor that he was going to do a remake of an old Jimmy Stewart film, "Mr. Smith Goes To Washington" (a film against Congressional corruption and apathy.) But that hasn't worked out.

There's also a thought of having John star in a film about Johnny Appleseed, the folklore hero who went around the country, spreading appleseeds, from which grew vast apple orchards. His agent, Jerry Weintraub, is also listening to other movie ideas and reading scripts that might fit John's personality.

In his steady climb to success, John has had many high points—the first million-seller, the first big concerts, his first big TV special. In January 1976, there was still another show business summit for him.

Each year, the members of AGVA, the American Guild of Variety Artists (a labor union that works to protect show business performers) choose outstanding "Live" entertainers to receive awards. The sixth annual AGVA Awards, broadcast over CBS-TV, took place in Caesar's Palace in Las Vegas. Jackie Gleason was host, and among those who appeared were Telly Savalas of "Kojack" fame, George Burns, Lucille Ball, Jimmy Walker and Gabe Kaplan of ABC's "Welcome Back, Kotter." Like most of these award shows, the program itself was rather dull and unimaginative. But the awards mean something because they are made by performers themselves as a "salute to live performers." Winners receive statuettes called "Georgies," named after the vaudeville star-songwriter-actor-producer George M. Cohan of years ago.

John Denver won a "Georgie" as "Top Male Singer of the Year."

John couldn't be there. In a taped message shot outdoors, amidst leafy beauty, John told the TV audience: "I love making records. I love doing television. I love diving into the sea with Captain Cousteau and climbing mountains and everything. Just about the most meaningful thing in my life is to be up in front of people to share my music with them."

John has it all. Million-selling records, awards, TV specials, work he enjoys, a beautiful home, a beautiful wife, and a family. "My life is perfect," he says, "I wouldn't change a thing."

DISCOGRAPHY, SONGBOOKS, TV, FILMS, AWARDS

Albums

Beginnings John Denver with Mitchell Trio (Mercury)
Poems, Prayers, Promises
Rhymes and Reasons
Take Me To Tomorrow
Aerie
Whose Garden Was This?
Farewell Andromeda
Rocky Mountain High
Back Home Again
John Denver's Greatest Hits
Rocky Mountain Christmas
An Evening With John Denver
Sunshine (Sound-track, MCA)
Windsong

Million-Selling Singles

"Take Me Home, Country Roads"	(1971)
"Rocky Mountain High"	(1973)
"Sunshine On My Shoulder"	(1974)
"Annie's Song"	(1974)
"I'm Sorry"	(1975)
"Back Home Again"	(1975)

Million-Selling Albums

Poems, Prayers, Promises	(1971)
Aerie	(1972)
Rocky Mountain High	(1972)
Farewell Andromeda	(1973)
John Denver's Greatest Hits	(1973)
Back Home Again	(1974)
An Evening With John Denver	(1975)
Windsong	(1975)
Rocky Mountain Christmas	(1975)

Platinum Records

Million-sellers are those that sell a million dollars worth of records; tapes, cassettes. Platinum records are those albums (or singles) which actually sell a million copies and realize $5-6 million dollars at retail prices. A platinum single, of course, makes much less.

John Denver's Greatest Hits
Rocky Mountain High

Songbooks

Windsong—John Denver—Songs from the lp including "I'm Sorry," "Windsong."

An Evening With John Denver—Twenty-three songs.

The John Denver Songbook—Hits from four best-selling albums.

Back Home Again—John Denver—Includes "Annie's Song," "Thank God I'm a Country Boy," "Sweet Surrender."

Aerie—John Denver—Based on his lp.

Farewell Andromeda—John Denver—Songs from lp plus some from John's TV special "Big Horn."

Rocky Mountain High—John Denver—Including, of course, "Rocky Mountain High."

The Music of John Denver—Simplified Piano Arrangements.

T V Films
(Selected List)

"The First John Denver Picture Show"
"An Evening With John Denver"
"The John Denver Show"
"Rocky Mountain Christmas"
"The John Denver Show"—BBC-TV Series
"John Denver And A Friend"—A salute to the big bands with guest star Frank Sinatra.
"Big Horn Country"—ABC wild-life documentary, narration and music by John Denver.
"Sunshine"—CBS-TV film. John on soundtrack.
"The Bears And I"—Disney film. John composed and sang key song, "Sweet Surrender."

Awards

CMA (Country Music Association)	"Entertainer of the Year" Song of the Year: "Back Home Again" 1975
ASCAP Country Music Award	John Denver was honored with five awards, two as song-writer, and three as performer. 1975
Academy of Country Music	Album of the Year Award: *Back Home Again* 1975
Emmy Award	"An Evening With John Denver" ABC-TV 1975
AGVA (American Guild of Variety Artists)	Winner of "Georgie" as "Top Male Singer of the Year" 1976
The People's Choice Award	Only entertainment award selected by the public through a scientific sampling instead of by entertainers themselves. "Favorite Musical Performer" 1976